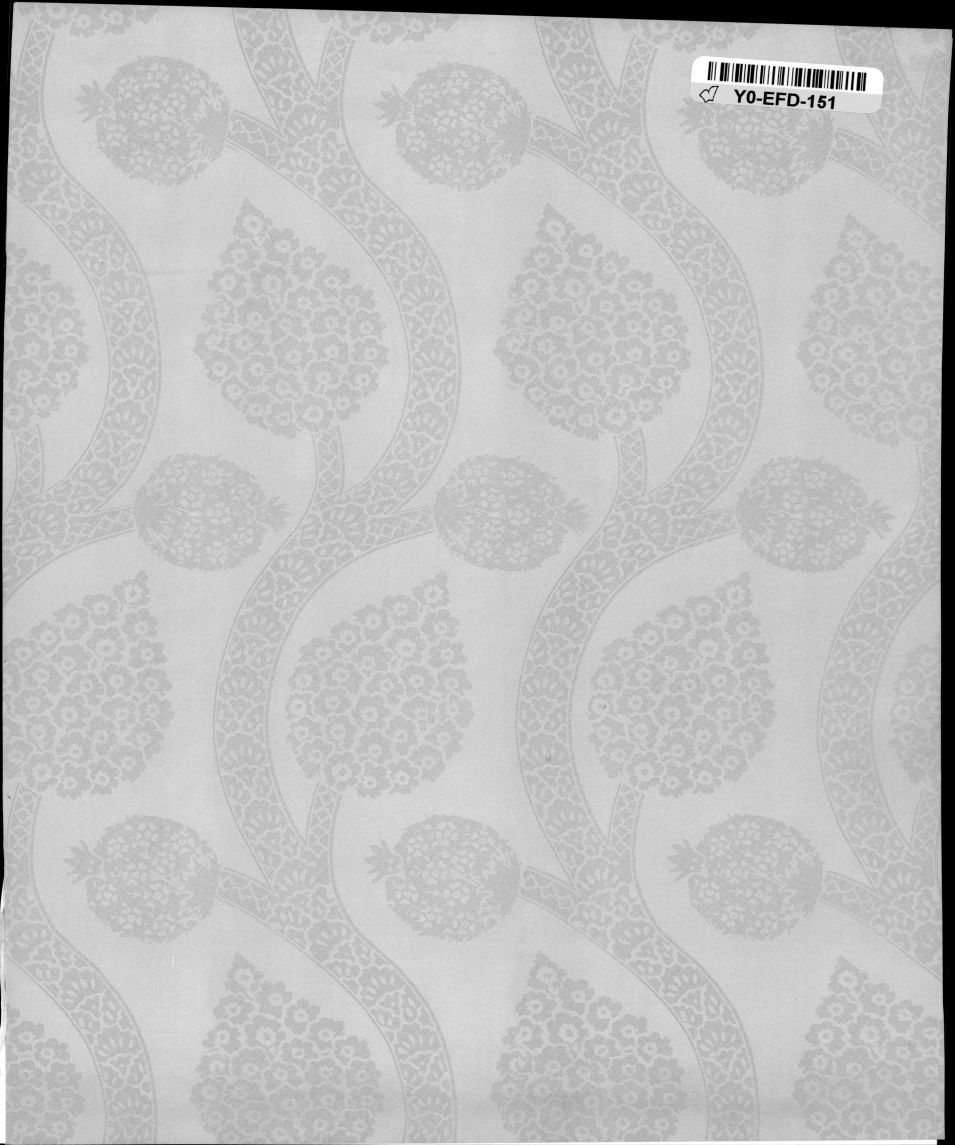

BETH WEBB
An Eye for Beauty

ROOMS THAT SPEAK TO THE SENSES

Written with Judith Nasatir
Foreword by Clinton Smith

RIZZOLI
NEW YORK

New York Paris London Milan

To my husband, Chuck,
love of my life: you were worth the wait.
And to Taylor and Graeme:
always follow your heart home.

Contents

Foreword

I have known Beth Webb for more than a decade. But, unknowingly, I wandered into her world long before that, when I happened to visit a project she had designed. (It was not until years after we met that I discovered she was the one responsible for it.)

Almost twenty years later, I recall walking into the space and thinking it felt like a breath of fresh air. But it was actually more like a blast of fresh thinking.

I don't consider Beth's work "Southern design"—it has a worldview—but the South is her home base, and her work embodies all the things Southerners love: kick-up-your-feet elegance, a blend of classic and contemporary, and a sense of place. She ushered in an era of bright and brilliant, ethereal interiors, without all the heavy trappings that often accompanied regional design work at the time. Now her style ethos has been exported from coast to coast and internationally, proving that the best design—regardless of where it originates—is timeless.

A soft palette is a continuous thread in her work, yet the craft of creating inviting rooms with subtle fabrics and quiet paint colors doesn't come easily. Combining neutrals in rooms that don't leave you cold or empty is both a science and an art. Beth is a master at marrying the two, resulting in resplendent spaces that are warm and inviting. The nuances are often indiscernible at first, but after a while, the little details that define her work shine through. And when you mix all of that with her passion for art, magic happens.

Beth also says yes. In addition to running a successful business, she is generous with her time. I have worked with her on countless charity projects over the years, to which she has lent her design expertise and talent, and each time I've requested her participation, there was never a hesitation. I value her generosity of spirit, especially in an age in which time is the greatest luxury. That spirit of saying yes extends to her clients, whose collections and wants and desires and dreams she welcomes with open arms, in turn giving them a design that delivers more than they ever wished for.

And every time I see a space that Beth has created, I see her reflection: happy, smart, spirited, clever, beautiful, fun, and elegant, yet down-to-earth. Lucky are the clients who get to work with her, and the readers who can now draw inspiration and ideas from this book.

—*Clinton Smith*

Coming Home

There are so many different kinds of homes, as many as there are people. But as for the way we want our homes to make us feel, I believe that's universal, and visceral. Once our deepest instincts assure us that we're safe in a given space, our higher senses kick in and we begin to absorb the atmosphere of our surroundings in a nuanced and layered way. Often, that complex sensual experience defies analysis. Yet that's precisely where design enters the picture, because design, especially for interiors, involves much that we can't see as well as the dazzling, beautiful things that we do.

The design process starts with life—and how we live. There is an art to living well, to elevating the everyday. This art is all-encompassing and sensual, and it begins with the properties of our environments that we can feel but not necessarily see or touch. Then come the aesthetics, which are as varied as we are. For me, the sensual takes precedence. It doesn't matter what the vernacular of the house is, whether it's formal, transitional, or rustic. What I want above all is for the interiors I create to imbue those who live in them with feelings of well-being and contentment.

For most of us, a love of home comes down to our personal traditions and rituals. These are very often ingrained and imparted at a very early age. Where we go, whom and what we love: all these experiences filter into what we do and who we are. Sunday suppers at my grandparents', my mother's Christmas lunch for fifty, Thanksgivings at the family farm in Alabama, where the number of dogs exceeds the number of people—these comprise the memories that inform my own sense of home.

I grew up surrounded by generations of family and close family friends in the tiny town of Lookout Mountain, Tennessee, with a population of 1,600. My mother had an inherent love of beauty. She knew quality. And she taught my sister and me to care about both. Yet our house, which stood on a wooded mountain lot, felt dark and uncomfortable.

So I have always craved light, and layers of light, for my own rooms and the homes I design for others. Light is essential to life, and it's one of my absolutes for transforming a house into a home. That's why the orientation of a house and its rooms matters so deeply. If there's a lack of natural light, I will figure out another way to create a luminous ambience. Light is a form of joy. No one can, or should, live without it.

When I think of all the sensual things that make a home feel warm and wonderful, I think of my grandparents' houses and how they lived in them. Growing up, I spent a lot of time with both sets of grandparents. Each of my grandmothers influenced my life profoundly. I would walk to their houses after school and stay with them most weekends as a child. My maternal grandparents' house was on the bluff, on the east brow of the mountain. My fondest memories are of waking up there, snug in a bed dressed with freshly ironed sheets, the warmth of the sun's rays dancing around the room, the clock ticking outside the door, the aromas of coffee, bacon, and toast (done correctly in the oven) perfuming the air, a mourning dove cooing outside the window—that house was full of the comforts of home. Most of my aesthetic sensibility I trace to my paternal grandmother. She taught me to knit, embroider, make chutney, and so much more—all the parts and pieces of the domestic arts that contribute to a gratifying life well lived. She had a wonderful sense of style and impeccable taste. So did many of the other women in my circle of family and friends, each of them an important influence in so many ways.

Life on the farm in Alabama taught me much about the elegance of simplicity, and what a rich model it can be for living well. Both a working farm and a hunting plantation, the farm is rustic, and so beautiful. Time stands still there. As my mother used to say, "Honey, this is Alabama. Slow down." Built in 1920, the main house, which we refer to as the clubhouse, consists of one main gathering room, a large dining room for family-style meals, and two bunkhouse wings off the main room—one for "setters" (girls) and one for "pointers" (boys). (It *is* a hunting lodge, after all.) The farm embodies a romanticized way of life that now is mostly lost to history. It's where my family has always gone, generation with generation. It's

the place my children love more than life itself. It has schooled us all in the grace of the South's agricultural tradition and the roots of what we consider Southern hospitality—and home.

My longing for that sanctuary that I call home has been with me all my life. Quiet, space, and serenity are what I seek each time I return home at the end of a crazy workday, or from a trip farther afield. My clients seek the same for themselves and their families. Yet for each of them, as for me, that ideal must find a unique, individual expression. The techniques, tools, and elements of interior design make it possible to create such places. Every home begins as a blank canvas: a plan, a way, and a structure to encapsulate life. Only through its materials, furnishings, and details does it become beautiful, comfortable, personal. In retrospect, I realize that I absorbed these ideas unconsciously simply through the process of growing up in the homes that formed my childhood universe. But my early education also played a fundamental role in learning to see beauty.

The mountain was an anomaly—tiny, but sophisticated. Strangely, there were a few local families who collected important American art. So while I didn't personally grow up with such fine things, I experienced them daily as a child. Art history, studio art, and French were intrinsic parts of our school curriculum from kindergarten all the way through high school. I still have the little art history notebook that they handed out to us in kindergarten. Every week they would give us another postcard, illustrated with one of the great works of art—Gainsborough's *The Blue Boy*, Monet's *Water Lilies*, Manet's *Le Déjeuner sur l'herbe*, and so on through the canon—to save in our book. In high school, I was fortunate to have a wonderful art history teacher who became my mentor, spurring me to pursue a future in art and art history.

One of my earliest memories is of drawing—tracing, really—images from a book. My grandmother had come into the library while I had the book open. She stepped out and returned with tracing paper. Soon I was lying on the floor tracing, of all things, illustrations from Dante's *Inferno*. Those are not pretty pictures, especially for a small child, but I loved the line quality of the engravings. That volume is with me still, perched proudly among the design books on my living room coffee table.

During my junior year in college, I studied abroad in Canterbury, England. I've since realized that the most valuable part of my education during that time was in the travel, not so much the academics, because every weekend my friends and I were on a train headed somewhere else: Greece or Spain, Portugal or Paris, Morocco or Madrid.

Determined to move back to Europe after I graduated, at least for a while, I enrolled in the Sotheby's Works of Art course, a one-year program held in London. One of my most firmly held beliefs as a designer is "See it, touch it, feel it." I trace this back to the Sotheby's course because they drilled into us the motto "You learn by looking." Our main classrooms were the Victoria & Albert Museum and the great houses of Britain. We visited museums and country houses weekly and worked in the various departments at Sotheby's. We were permitted to touch everything, and to crawl under the furniture to ascertain how it was made. My eyes, already informed by years of looking, grew sharper and more discriminating. I began to develop and hone an instinctive sense of quality, of line, form, and composition. I learned that the senses, informed by experience—seeing, touching, feeling—are absolutely essential to connoisseurship of any kind. This experiential education is cumulative, even exponential.

When I finished at Sotheby's, I knew I wanted to live and work in New York, which was the epicenter of the art world at the time. After a stint at a prominent New York art gallery, followed by a return to the South, I ended up dealing privately. I often hung art in my house so that the clients might see it in a residential setting. I also entertained frequently. One night, one of my dinner guests—a childhood friend—suggested I consider taking up a new challenge. He informed the table that the foundation with which he worked had just purchased an 1892 house. "We're looking for an interior designer," he said. Turning to me, he added, "And I think you should do it." I told him I wasn't a decorator. He responded, "But you could be." He suggested that I pull together some photos of interiors that appealed to me and make a presentation. The foundation had a major collection of photography, so because of the way art segues into interior design, he thought it would be the perfect transition for me to blend one with the other. I had always been obsessed with shelter magazines (I still am). So I assembled a portfolio of sorts (which even today sits on a shelf in my office) to show inspirational ideas illustrated by work from my betters, including Nancy Braithwaite and Stephen Sills.

The only direction the foundation's officers gave me when they offered me the job was to keep to the look of the portfolio I had presented. And so I did, because the spirit of the images I had chosen expressed my ideals for what a home, at its best, should be: spacious and light-filled; gracious and welcoming; functional to a fault but with the elegance of simplicity; expressive of personality but visually quiet, deeply calm, and rich in comfort. To this day, these are the qualities I believe make a house feel like a home.

The foundation threw a gala to show off its new offices, and that led to my second project, a 30,000-square-foot 1920s Tudor. It was a dream job, but it came with unenviable time constraints: the project had to be completed within eight weeks. I somehow accomplished that, outfitting the house without a hitch. And by the time I did, I had become an interior designer.

In the years since then, I have created numerous homes for myself, my family, and my clients. Each has reflected the personalities within, as they were at that particular phase of life. Each has combined some remembrances of things past with things beloved in the moment and treasured for the future. With all of life's twists and turns, I have continued to discover not just the infinite nuances of the interior designer's art and profession, but also how deep the psychological connections are to what I do and how I do it. With that, I have also learned how powerful design can be.

An idea of home is visceral, but we can truly share it only when we make it tangible— when we can see it, touch it, feel it. Then, and only then, do we know that we're home.

sight

Our eyes are first among equals as far as our five senses are concerned. Sight not only leads us into our experience of the world around us, it also has the power to enhance or diminish all our other sensual responses, both on first glance and with extended viewing. And since each of us sees in our own way, how we see is utterly intrinsic to who we are.

I believe one learns by looking. Our critical faculties and our aesthetic sensibilities are constantly informed by a barrage of visual stimulation. The most inspiring for me is travel; the more exotic, the better—think the Great Pyramids, the souks of Marrakech, the Greek isles. By taking me out of my comfort zone of home, travel brings the world into sharper focus. As a result, I see things differently. And as I subconsciously internalize these experiences, they become a part of who I am as a designer.

Because of my background in fine art—and my passion for drawing—line takes precedence in my point of view. I honor line, form, structure, and composition as the key animators and activators of space, and as algorithms for creating beauty. In the same way that an artist looks at a blank canvas, I approach the design of a space first through its linear elements, via a graphic assessment. Then I layer the components of living on top of those foundational lines.

Form is sensuality. Curves beckon. Straight edges, definitive as they are, beg for the contrast of undulating lines. Balancing the two is the constant of composition. From that perspective, a wing chair, for instance, becomes a sculptural piece even more so than a utilitarian one. I see it, in and of itself, as a work of art, one that then must relate in form and scale to its nearby neighbors in an overall seating arrangement and to all the rest of the room's pieces, both functional and decorative.

The eye, in my experience, tends more often than not to move across, up, and down as it travels in a room. This knowledge affects spatial planning down to the last compositional detail. What do I want people to see? How do I direct the eye to move around the room? In terms of shapes, relationships, and the massing of objects and furniture pieces, I tend to think in triangles (the eye moving across, up, and down). From years of art installations, I've learned that if a particular piece, no matter how small, is powerful enough, it can command a wall. The same truth exists for furniture elements, objects, and decorative accessories. The air around each and every object is key, as are odd numbers in groupings.

Color, to me, is in many ways a matter of economics, longevity, and, moreover, simplicity. Our tastes and sensibilities inevitably change with age and experience. Understated building blocks allow an interior to transition almost at will as that happens. If the larger pieces in our rooms wear a neutral exterior, then it is possible—and comparatively easy—to update a space with art, decorative pillows, floor coverings, and window treatments that reflect our latest passions and preferences.

No room, no home, should give up all the secrets of its décor to prying eyes on a first date—nuance is the reward of extended viewing. Subtlety, to my mind, plays a profound role in the layering that timeless decoration requires.

A decorative trim on the lead edge of a drapery panel or the simplest flange on the edge of a seat cushion—so many exquisite details may be almost indiscernible when one first surveys the room as a whole, but their revelation over time is one of the most beautiful aspects of design.

PAGE 16: A perfectly proportioned room gratifies all the senses, as is the case with this library in a historically significant Atlanta house from the 1920s. A soft lime-wash finish on original wood paneling and a textural palette of neutral hues refresh the room's inherent beauty. OPPOSITE: A completely integrated composition of forms, colors, and materials will draw interest to a far corner. FOLLOWING PAGES, LEFT: With understated sparkle, a quartz crystal lamp always provides an intriguing, dramatic flourish. FOLLOWING PAGES, RIGHT: When tradition meets modernity in a room with great architecture, the effect is completely captivating.

Love at First Glance

In a quest for the American dream, perfect is as perfect does, especially where a family's forever home is concerned. These clients yearned for a house with a significant historical heritage in which to raise their three young children. Specifically, they wanted a property designed by one of Atlanta's great twentieth-century architects, Philip Trammell Shutze (1890–1982). When their architect, Stan Dixon, introduced me to them, they were already midway through the search that yielded their quintessential Shutze estate: a 1920s Georgian Revival brick house on five beautifully landscaped acres.

The home's former owners had extended the first-floor living spaces with a master bedroom suite, family room, and breakfast room. But the prior renovations were done in an English-country-house fashion that was just too traditional for this young family. They wanted a house that thrummed with life and light, made the most of the house's spectacular bones, and honored the architect's original intentions. So as we reenvisioned the interiors, we referred to Shutze's original blueprints, which Dixon had found, and we added back original elements that were previously lost.

With classic, expansive graciousness, the rooms flow from a dramatic foyer with superb 1920s architectural detailing through the primary living areas to the private spaces. The entry sits on axis with the loggia and garden, so the very first view on crossing the threshold is through to the manicured grounds beyond. The dining room, kitchen, and butler's pantry extend off one side of the foyer; the living room and library off the other. Past the powder room, a stair descends to a hallway that leads on one side to the master suite and on the other to the family room.

My client is very definitive about what she loves and what she feels passionate about, especially as far as art and antiques are concerned. So we worked closely together to create the

PREVIOUS PAGES: A black lacquer Art Deco-inspired chest with sleek notes of Lucite and blown glass sets the tone for a foyer done in graphic black and white. RIGHT: Interjections of midcentury modern furnishings and contemporary abstract art help bring the neoclassical architecture of the living room up to date. A compositional palette of creams, grays, and golds accentuates the architectural positives. The Greek key motif on the drapery panels recurs throughout the house.

antiques-meets-modern, contemporary-playing-well-with-historical style that she desired. In the living room, a luminous palette of caramel, taupe, cognac, and pale gray creates an elegant, refined setting with a translucent glow. Contemporary drawings and abstract art feel right at home amid the carefully curated arrangements of midcentury modern and antique furnishings.

In the dining room, we consciously strayed from the interior's let-there-be-light motif with bittersweet chocolate-colored walls, an antique crystal chandelier, and subtly patterned drapery panels. Following Shutze's original plans, the architect reintroduced the mirrored transoms. The inclusion of a midcentury bar cabinet further enhanced the room's ambience.

We redesigned the formerly dark kitchen to bring it up to date. A combination of open shelving and closed cabinetry echoes its 1920s origins, while a zinc and nickel custom range hood, a new central island, and porcelain subway wall tiles offer both function and brightness. As a final touch, we painted the dark wood floor in a graphic black-and-white grid pattern.

With walls in a changeling pale blue-green, the master bedroom subtly shifts character and hue throughout the day under a cloud-like lime-washed ceiling. Mirrored vanities, a fluted wall, black-lacquered cabinetry, and a book-matched marble floor infuse the master bath with timeless glamour.

Full of light, redesigned for today's lifestyle but honoring the past, too, this wonderful homage to Atlanta's architectural history now embodies the owner's dream of home—and in that way, it's as perfect as perfect can be.

The transom above the door reproduces one of Schutze's intended components, which architect Stan Dixon discovered in the house's original plans.

There's a method to the madness of the dining room's color scheme. During a dinner party, the depth and density of the chocolate walls envelop the host and guests with warm, luxurious intimacy. Plus, what could be more dramatic than the delicious contrast of those walls with the pale velvet of the upholstery fabric? The mirrored transom over the door reproduces an original element removed in an earlier remodel; it adds necessary height to the doorway and restores the room's architectural balance.

ABOVE AND OPPOSITE: Reformatted in bright white, the fresh, modern kitchen feels a bit like a throwback to the original, but better. The crisp black-and-white painted grid of the floor serves as a great foundation for the shimmer of walls lined with subway tile and counters of Calacatta marble. FOLLOWING PAGES, LEFT: In a bay in the master bedroom, a mirrored table adds a touch of 1920s glamour. FOLLOWING PAGES, RIGHT: Windowed on two walls, a sitting room off the master bedroom also serves as a sunroom.

ABOVE AND OPPOSITE: For those of us who consider the master bedroom the most important room in the house, it should be a sanctuary—soothing for the eyes and mind and luxuriously comfortable above all. This bedroom's quiet palette of soft colors is enlivened by understated textures and patterns, including touches of the Greek key motif that threads its way throughout the interior.

OPPOSITE: The master bathroom blends some truly traditional elements, like a book-matched marble floor, with a tightly edited group of very modern components, such as a custom glass shower door. The mirrored vanity (one of a pair) introduces an ultraglamorous note that harks back to Hollywood in the 1920s. ABOVE: A sculptural, artisan-made steel stool contrasts with the highly polished freestanding tub, which nestles into a niche framed by a fluted wall.

Sight Lines

Very often a family retreat at the lake, at the shore, or in the mountains proves to be that special place where family happiness dwells through the generations. When you are lucky enough to initiate your children into the traditions of such a place, one that you loved as a child, you see present desires meet future dreams. I am sure that this particular kind of alchemy inspired this couple to build their family's summer cottage on Walloon Lake in Michigan (where Hemingway summered as a child). Enlisting the help of Atlanta architect Peter Block, the couple developed the kind of rich interior architecture that sets the stage for lasting memories.

This summerhouse opens to nature in a spectacularly generous fashion. Directly on axis with the back, the front entrance greets guests with a gorgeous view of the lake. The entry hallway proceeds into a dramatic two-story living room with a massive stone fireplace and a butterfly stair on both interior walls, which balances the two-story screened-in porch on the lake-facing perimeter.

When views are as transfixing as these, I want to create rooms that complement them, not compete with them. And because this is a second home, it made sense to keep the details of decoration rather pared down. For those reasons, patina and texture became the main elements in setting the interior atmosphere. A lime wash colors all the walls (paneled in Douglas fir), moldings, trim, and floors a whispery, taupey green and seems to soften the surfaces, adding depth, touchability, and the illusion of age to create a sense of greater intimacy. Along with the stained woodwork, walls in shades of gentle China White allow the world beyond the windows to speak for itself. Much of the rest of the color palette derives from the lake itself, the landscape, and the light that reflects off the water into the interior.

Throughout these spaces, texture plays upon texture in tonal harmony. Both the main spaces and private areas of the house bask in dappled light from sunrise until the gloaming, when the night sky and stars take over. We designed and sized the furnishings for comfort (their scale was critical because the rooms are so capacious). The living room has welcoming upholstery at its core, a well-stocked bar, and a spectacular view of the lake below. The adjacent dining room, brilliantly windowed on two sides, feels as if it's in nature yet graciously sheltered from it at the same time.

To add intimacy in the sizable kitchen, we washed the cabinetry with a warm limed finish. The two islands were a solution to the need to accommodate both food preparation and casual dining in a single space.

Because of its high ceilings and ample windows, the master bedroom feels awash in air and light. To induce a sense of nesting, we incorporated a niche to cocoon the bed. Opposite, a seating area overlooks the lake, with linen panels acting as soft filters at the window. In the master suite and in the other bedrooms throughout the house, sumptuous down pillows, fabulous sheeting, and lofty duvets dress the bed; layers can be added or pared down season by season.

The textural play and tonal harmony respond to the surroundings all year round. In ten feet of snow, the cottage feels like a Swiss chalet. In mid-July, with doors and windows flung open to the summer breezes, it's an American dream home, all Norman Rockwell and cherry pie.

PREVIOUS PAGES: Built on a gorgeous waterfront site and nestled into the native pines, this house pays homage to the landscape by framing spectacular views of Walloon Lake and the surrounding woods from every room. In season, there's nothing more relaxing than a catnap in this hammock overlooking the lake. OPPOSITE: Cozy and intimate, the dining room feels as if it's actually in the woods thanks to two enormous window walls.

RIGHT: Framed by lime-washed wood planks, the foyer
offers a warm welcome and opens to the main living area.
FOLLOWING PAGES, LEFT: Organic textures fill the house,
infusing it with understated pattern and subtle,
neutral colors. FOLLOWING PAGES, RIGHT: The mud hall
becomes a drop zone for the necessary odds and
ends of everyday living, so its decoration includes all the
accoutrements for proper storage, hidden neatly.

On the side of the double-height living room that looks through to the dining room, a major seating group focuses on the massive stone hearth (we pulled the room's color palette straight from its gradation of hues). A custom cabinet houses the TV.

With one island outfitted for prep work and the other for seating (it often serves as a breakfast table), the double island configuration maximizes the kitchen's functionality and flexibility. Bookending one of the kitchen sinks is a pair of tall cabinets: one houses the refrigerator; the other, additional storage. The lantern pendants add necessary overhead light, while a variation of the same lime-wash finish used elsewhere in the house transforms the wood cabinetry with its soft patina.

PREVIOUS PAGES, LEFT: In the intimate library, custom his-and-hers desks back up to a dramatic view of the lake. Lime-washed paneling gives the room a radiant glow. Convenient shelving houses books and collections. Each double-sided desk allows the sitter the choice of facing toward or away from the view. PREVIOUS PAGES, RIGHT: A pair of small club chairs and ottomans offers cozy lounge seating—perfect for reading a book or for a conversational interlude in front of the small fireplace. RIGHT: In the master suite, which is organized around the views, the head of the bed tucks into a niche designed for that very purpose. Quiet and monochromatic (but with a tone or two drawn from the waters of the lake beyond), the subdued color palette provides a calming background for the natural setting. Linen textiles in different densities and hefts tell a textural story that adds understated visual interest. Dressed in many layers, the bed adapts easily for different seasons.

OPPOSITE: A windowed bay in the master bedroom outfitted with cozy, comfortable seating provides a perfect getaway spot for spending time with a favorite novel or in peaceful contemplation. Floor-to-ceiling linen panels filter the light and frame the view. ABOVE: The warm patina of lime-washed, wood-paneled walls infuses the master bath with tactility, depth, and elegance. His-and-hers vanities flank the doorway. Silver travertine provides a beautiful, cool surface underfoot.

RIGHT: With two queen beds, a pair of club chairs, and a desk, the daughter's room works well for a multitude of guests. She wanted all her friends to be able to share her room for slumber parties, so it sleeps five (the window seat is a twin) and can accommodate more when desired. FOLLOWING PAGES, LEFT: In an upstairs guest bedroom, an indoor shutter injects an air of unexpected charm. FOLLOWING PAGES, RIGHT: The tub in the master bath takes advantage of the gorgeous views.

sound

We live our lives out loud and in surround sound. The joyful noise of the human voice is one of our first stimuli in the process of getting to know the world around us. As individual as a fingerprint, and definitive in range, rhythm, and accent, our voice says who we are and so much more. And we prick up our ears in response not only to our own human babble but also to the constant barrage of the world's complex aural landscape. These auditory clues, both man-made and natural, cue us in to the surrounding context and affect our experience of time and place. Every city has its particular din, and every office its particular hum. The cadence of the waves varies from Atlantic to Pacific, from Adriatic to Aegean, on rocky coasts or sandy beaches, in storms or calm seas. A wind can whisper, whistle, or whine through trees, between buildings, around a house. Birdsong is as specific and regional as every other idiom of vocal expression. And so on, ad infinitum.

Auditory quality is an essential aspect of interior personality, for sound directly affects the way we know home and the pleasure and comfort that we take in it. Yet each home generates its own distinctive form of chamber music, a unique acoustical world that is intrinsic to its identity and completely separate from that which is created by an audiophile's beloved equipment. Such is the melody of memory. The creak of a step, the sound of a foot-fall muffled by a plush rug or resounding on stone, the swish of a curtain panel, the thrum of a faucet, the chime of a doorbell—all these and so many more rate as classics on a built-in residential sound track. The art of creating a sense of place encompasses this aural dimension, and our material choices affect the overall tapestry—and decibel level—of the distinctive domestic sounds that we associate with the idea of home.

We take in acoustical information instinctively and analytically. Sound is a physical thing—a matter of waves of various frequencies that strike corresponding chords in our nervous systems. Each place has its own distinctive set of aural cues, every home its particular quiet roar. Much of that has to do with the personalities within a family and the way they interact with one another. If only walls could talk. . . . If only walls had ears. . . .

The sounds of life are all around us.
They reside in the elements
of design and are intrinsic
to the comforts we call home.

PREVIOUS PAGES: The sound of the surf reaching the beach is truly nature's music. When a house is just steps away, the tidal rhythms become an integral part of the home's environment. OPPOSITE: A courtyard pool with a flowing fountain provides a delightful (and cooling) accompaniment all day and night to the rooms that surround it. FOLLOWING PAGES, LEFT: Exotic flora lend a sense of place that is its own form of enchantment. Their leaves often rustle in a distinctive background whisper. FOLLOWING PAGES, RIGHT: An alcove adjacent to the pool offers a peaceful respite from the blazing sun of the tropics.

Call of the Wild

Travel sharpens all the senses. For me, it is the best way to tune in to inspiration in order to focus on any pressing matters at hand. Each time I arrive in Las Catalinas, Costa Rica, I find I listen more intently (and taste, smell, see, and touch, too). The aural tapestry here is so distinctive—from the sounds of the surf to the cacophony of the parakeets, from the roar of the howler monkeys to the sotto voce of the courtyard fountains—it reminds me afresh how integral the soundscape is to what designers like to call "context." Here, homes make the most of indoor/outdoor relationships. Sound plays a major role in this dynamic. Layering in man-made features to supplement nature's accompaniment is part of what makes the process of creating home interiors so sensually appealing.

When the couple brought me into this project, it was still under construction: the exteriors were complete and the rooms were framed, but the floors hadn't been laid and the bathrooms and kitchens had yet to be designed. With a mere two months to ready the spaces for use, we determined the aesthetic palette, choosing all the materials, finishes, and decorative elements with the utmost practicality.

She requested that all the rooms—both indoors and out—be fresh, light, and airy. For the fabrics and finishes, we opted for varying shades of white with blues because the combination is so cooling in the brilliant sun and so right for the seaside. To give the white spaces visual interest and make them feel welcoming, we introduced layer upon layer of texture, including all sorts of woven materials from linen to wicker and rattan.

Because indoor/outdoor dining is a major component of the Las Catalinas lifestyle, it was important to design an adaptable dining area within the living space so that particular area can serve a variety of purposes. We curtained the outdoor dining terrace to suggest a semblance of privacy since the houses in this walkable community are set so close together. When the curtain luffs and billows in the breeze, it creates both an illusion of air-conditioning and its own background music.

The airy feeling continues in the kitchen, which has open shelving finished in a pale washed gray. Concrete tiles made on the property pave the walls and floors and keep the room feeling cool even in the ever-present tropical heat.

One of the loveliest features of this house is a waterfall set into the side of the pool. It generates a constant, soothing stream of water—all in all, a gentle beguilement that greets the couple when they wake and provides a lullaby at night.

PREVIOUS PAGES: An outpost of the New Urbanism movement, Las Catalinas is a car-free community. Residents walk and bike through the quaint, quiet pathways. OPPOSITE: Dark-stained wood and white plaster are key to the local architectural vocabulary. From the second floor landing, the stair descends in a graceful profile of curves.

PAGE 70: Driftwood at the tide line adds its sculptural beauty to the upper reaches of the beach. PAGE 71: The living room opens on one side to the pool courtyard; on the other, to the dining area. Inviting textures beckon, and a blue, white, and natural palette feels cooling. PREVIOUS PAGES: The courtyard pool has a built-in bench for those who live to be half in, half out of the water. Rattan cushions are perfect for wet swimsuits. ABOVE AND OPPOSITE: The kitchen takes its color palette from the rest of the house.

PREVIOUS PAGES: Apart from a vintage rattan chair, the bedroom furniture was crafted locally. The bolster is a wake-up call to pattern. ABOVE: With a sectional sofa and hassocks, the playroom offers many seating options. OPPOSITE: In the bunkroom, drawers are integrated into the stair risers. FOLLOWING PAGES, LEFT: Bold graphic elements bring a liveliness to this bedroom. FOLLOWING PAGES, RIGHT: In the front hall, a painted floorcloth introduces the blue-and-white motif. Mercury glass lamps add just enough shimmer.

Blue Notes

Whenever I am decorating a home by a lake, at the beach, or in the mountains, I make sure to savor the sounds that fill the air. The snap of pine needles underfoot. The whisper of leaves rustling in the breeze. The lap of water against the shore. The crackle and hiss of burning logs in the hearth. Almost invariably, the homeowners request a peaceful, gracious retreat that embraces this aspect of the atmosphere, that heightens the relationship between the interior and its surroundings. From my perspective, that means using the elements of design to gently tease all the senses, from visual to tactile to aural. What's wonderful is that so many materials, furnishings, fabrics, and accessories exist to accomplish that. As a result, these choices can now always be as personal as they are contextual. This light-infused lake home, for example, sits up above Lake Oconee, in the heart of one of Georgia's most beautiful rural landscapes. The client, who wanted to honor the breathtakingly dramatic views from every interior vantage point, happens to love the color blue in all its various shades, from watery to crisp to whispery. What better choice could there have been than to tailor the rooms around her preferred palette, seeing as it inherently emphasizes the interior-exterior connection?

The soaring living room opens onto a spacious porch that embraces the landscape and views of the lake, while a bay window frames a different perspective. Essentially neutral, the palette in the living area provides a still, calm, and quiet spatial canvas where curves beckon and texture creates pattern. Here and there, pops of blue punctuate the interior vistas and draw the eye outward toward the water. Playing off the palette of blues and neutrals here and elsewhere throughout the interiors allows a harmonious visual flow from room to room. By the same token, the wash of blue tones within the house helps turn a collection of disparate rooms into a seamlessly integrated whole.

PREVIOUS PAGES: A custom leaded mirror introduces a reference to history atop a painted Swedish chest. RIGHT: In the living room, texture clearly creates its own bold language of pattern. The broad linen stripes layer in a strong graphic grammar that helps to tie the elements of the room together. Symmetry also helps to quiet down the visual riot to an urbane level, as does the muted palette of neutrals, blues, and whites. On the mantel, a pair of antique finials adds the charm and patina of age into the eclectic mix.

While the owner wanted the rooms to feel fresh, casual, and friendly, she also loves layered décor. To create a satisfying richness and patina, we incorporated numerous antiques, including an incredible cabinet that anchors one wall of the dining room and houses various pieces from her collection of blue-and-white porcelain. Comfortable wicker chairs, so conducive to lake living, surround the dining table and help imbue the space with a relaxed sensibility. While the chandelier adds a necessary exclamation point overhead, we included lamps, sconces, and candles to provide layers of light and allow her to vary the ambience as she chooses for all times of day and a variety of occasions. I'm a great believer in multiple light sources, which help to create a psychological warmth that overhead lighting alone doesn't always deliver.

The family room centers on a stone fireplace, often lit and adding to the interior soundscape. With the juxtaposition of a heavily textured rug, linen-covered chairs, and an assemblage of baskets, there's a harmony of tactile and auditory qualities from rugged to refined to rustic.

Textural drama takes over the master bedroom with a play of caning against wicker, and lime-washed woods serve as counterpoints to the array of fabrics on the bed and at the window. With the sounds and sights of nature all around, what could be fresher?

OPPOSITE: On a bleached coffee table with an incised pattern and a great patina, blue-and-white ceramics look particularly vivid. The tones of the hydrangea blend right in, while the African beads provide a wonderful contrast. FOLLOWING PAGES, LEFT: On a stone-topped breakfast table, a chunky woven tray plays nicely with glassware in wicker sleeves. FOLLOWING PAGES, RIGHT: Massed in an oversized bouquet, hydrangea blooms have sculptural appeal.

PREVIOUS PAGES, LEFT: In a stone bowl, alabaster fruit takes on an exceptional glow. PREVIOUS PAGES, RIGHT: The underlying design motif here is a recurring play on form: the arched legs of the side table, the base of the antique sofa table, the Palladian window, and the ornament on the shoulders of the urns. RIGHT: Polished silver goblets and flatware raise the sophistication level of the table setting. Flanking a Swedish bibliothèque, pedestals topped by substantial urns infuse the room with power and presence.

ABOVE: The gentle creak of the headboard's caning and the rustle of the various linens help to orchestrate the beginning and end of each day with the welcome of quiet comfort. OPPOSITE: Soft blues enhance the bedroom's hushed, bleached tones.

touch

Touch me. Touch me not. Such is the primal binary system through which we filter our responses to the physical world within (and beyond) our immediate reach. The nature and quality of the tactile dictates the degree and character of comfort we feel.

Along with an educated eye, an experienced hand plays an essential role in the process of assessing and arbitrating quality and authenticity (as well as in the art and craft of creating things of beauty). In design, seeing isn't all there is to believing. Again, that is why I adhere to the mantra "See it, touch it, feel it." How else does one explore objects and materials to the point of comprehension, much less of connoisseurship? The approach holds true for stone, wood, and fabric, and whatever else it is that factors into the created environment, whether it comes into direct contact with any part of the body or merely contributes to the architectural surroundings. How sleek is that particular sleek? How rustic is that instance of rustic? Only by discovering the physical personality of each given patina, finish, and surface is it possible to verify whether it is really as pleasing and inviting as the eye suggests.

I love working with texture, layers and layers of texture. For me, design drama depends so much on the dimensional elements. I prefer to use the tactile components rather than the color palette to energize each space: a zebra rug, say, on top of sisal or nubby bouclé wool, snuggling up to a coarse Belgian linen. A smooth velvet or mohair against a lime-washed or waxed wood balances, contrasts, and harmonizes with a room's other dimensional surfaces and introduces visual interest into an otherwise monochromatic space. Texture creates pattern, albeit quiet pattern, which lends support to the peacefulness of the space while invigorating it, too.

The tactile aspect of comfort involves far more than just surface texture, especially where upholstered pieces are concerned. One person's ideal sofa or club chair is another's purgatory. When considering upholstery options for my clients, I'm rather insistent that they perform the sit test because body language reveals all. Some people sit up straight as a poker, while others collapse into the sofa.

And who could possibly choose fabrics from a photograph? We may see something we think we like, but before deciding to buy, we must experience a fabric by touching and caressing it, and feeling the texture against the skin. Cashmere, velvet, suede, and silk charmeuse: all of these and so many other fabrics beg to be handled and judged on a tactile level.

When it comes to comfort, quality is worth the wait. And its pursuit is also one of the best reasons that, as a designer, I will always travel. In today's world, so many of us slake our thirst for beauty on the Internet, where exceptional items, especially vintage and antique pieces, seem to be just a click away. But falling for an image without seeing, touching, and feeling the object in question can lead to an unhappy surprise when it arrives. When I am on the road, I always attempt to visit as many dealers as I can to get to know them and the quality of their wares firsthand.

The tactile is an absolute benchmark of design, and seminal to the feeling that is home. Touch me. Touch me not.

PREVIOUS PAGES: The juxtaposition of contrasts heightens all of our senses, touch included. In that way, baby's breath feels lacier and more delicate when offset by a gutsy wool carpet and the peeling finish of an antique iron urn. FOLLOWING PAGES, LEFT: The rusted finish of an antique cremone bolt adds a fascinating layer of patina to a bakery cabinet that incorporates reclaimed Belgian windows. FOLLOWING PAGES, RIGHT: A substantial late-nineteenth-century English oak table provides the keynote in this capacious formal dining room for a young family that loves to entertain.

Soft Focus

When the interior palette is monochromatic, and especially when it's predominantly white, textural variety must create the layers and juxtapositions that captivate the eye. But in a family home with an active toddler, like this gloriously luminous residence in Ponte Vedra, Florida, the all-white spaces must not only induce the requisite sense of quiet calm but also work hard to endure. So the tactile elements—all of the materials and finishes—take on extra, and extremely practical, dimensions.

The husband, a builder, designed and constructed this house, which sits on a deeply wooded lot surrounded by palmettos. His wife has a very clean-lined and edited aesthetic, and knew precisely where she wanted to go with the design process, but she needed help honing her choices and making sure she was on track with her vision. Our goal was to create rooms that felt as young, casual, and warm as the couple is. They wanted to accommodate the entertaining that they love and do so frequently. But it was critical that their interiors function well for their evolving family.

The floor plan placed all the heavy lifting, as far as daily activity goes, on the first floor, where all the main living areas spin organically off the central foyer. Instead of a formal living room, the couple opted for a huge family room, a logical choice for life with a toddler. Consequently, at the base of the central stair in the foyer we decided to create an intimate and more elegant seating area that serves a variety of purposes. (It comes in handy when guests join the family.)

VANITY FAIR 100 YEARS

The breakfast room, a section of the kitchen, flows into the family room, which includes upholstered pieces that are perfect for lounging and playing. In these spaces, beauty is paramount, but functionality is too. So when selecting the pieces, tactile surfaces—and their durability—were our major concern. For example, when we chose the breakfast-room table, we asked, "How's it going to handle cereal, sippy cups, and juice boxes?"

Indoors, the couple wanted a formal dining room that could seat up to fourteen, which made the size of the antique English oak table and its adaptability key. Outside, the family often uses the pool terrace for dinner parties, throwing open the French doors from the living room foyer and embracing the indoor/outdoor experience.

For this social pair, it was important that the master bedroom and its sitting room serve as both retreat and sanctuary. Here, we really emphasized the textural contrast, layering shades of white and off-white in an array of textiles and materials from highly refined to more rustic. Along with an understated play of subtle pattern, the various tactile elements contribute to an ethereal, sensual, harmonious effect.

In the end, these all-white (or almost all-white) rooms full of pragmatically beautiful elements do exactly what they ought to do: create opportunities for gracious family living, with all it entails.

PREVIOUS PAGES: Because this young family uses their family room as the go-to space for everyday activities, we created an elegant living area in the foyer for dressier occasions. The velvet-covered sofa backs up to a massive steel window frame set with mirrored panes. OPPOSITE: Functional and decorative, the seating area in the foyer serves beautifully for small get-togethers as well as for overflow at large parties. FOLLOWING PAGES, LEFT: The family room is this home's beating heart. Layering artworks creates visual interest and depth of field. FOLLOWING PAGES, RIGHT: My rule of three is in play with this compositional triangle of white vessels.

HORST **Photographer** *of* **Style**

OLAF HEINE BRAZIL

LONDON INTERIORS

PORTRAITS OF THE RENAISSAN

Windsor Smith HOMEFRONT

PIET BOON 1

A nineteenth-century European trunk
lends the family room a feeling of
history; its rustic texture and finish
are in keeping with other wood elements
in the space. A horizontal stripe on the
interior edge of the curtain panels introduces a subtle, unexpected element of
pattern. The upholstery is dressed in soft,
pale linens for comfort. Pillow fabrics
and knitted throws insert understated
pattern and textural nuance into the mix.

RIGHT: In the breakfast room bay, rattan chairs offer glimpses of the sculptural table base. Hefty in scale yet virtually transparent, a smoke bell lantern helps to establish intimacy in this ample space without weighing it down. FOLLOWING PAGES, LEFT: Quinces in a glass bowl on a bleached wood table: a harmonious meeting of refined, organic, and rustic. FOLLOWING PAGES, RIGHT: Decorative zinc architectural finials on bleached wood pedestals provide touches of whimsy and age.

ABOVE: In the gentleman's office, lime-washed shiplap panels establish a masculine mood. An antique Spanish basket brings a visible touch of the hand. OPPOSITE: Because he often works at home, his office had to be fully functional in every way. He is interested in design history, so he wanted furnishings that recall iconic pieces of the near and distant past.

In the all-white kitchen, varying textures and finishes along with understated metal and glass accents make all the difference. The subtle gray veining of a honed Calacatta marble backsplash imbues the room with a sense of motion. Glass vessels of different sizes and shapes on the counters, coupled with the glass cabinet doors and pendant lights over the island, provide reflection and the faintest suggestions of forms to activate the space.

ABOVE AND OPPOSITE: The contrast of rustic and refined brings a casual elegance to the tabletop. Woven rattan chargers contrast with classic white porcelain plates and set off the fineness of the linen napkins. Crystal stemware and glassware sparkle as they cast shape-shifting shadows atop a linen throw that doubles here as a table runner.

ABOVE AND OPPOSITE: In a guest room on the house's main level, the mélange of fabrics and textures takes soft, softer, and softest to the maximum in an exceptionally dreamy tone-on-tone palette. Linen drapery columns frame the window and bring verticality and appropriate scale to the space. From the curtain hardware to the bedframe to the stool bases, slender linear elements introduce graphic detail and dimension.

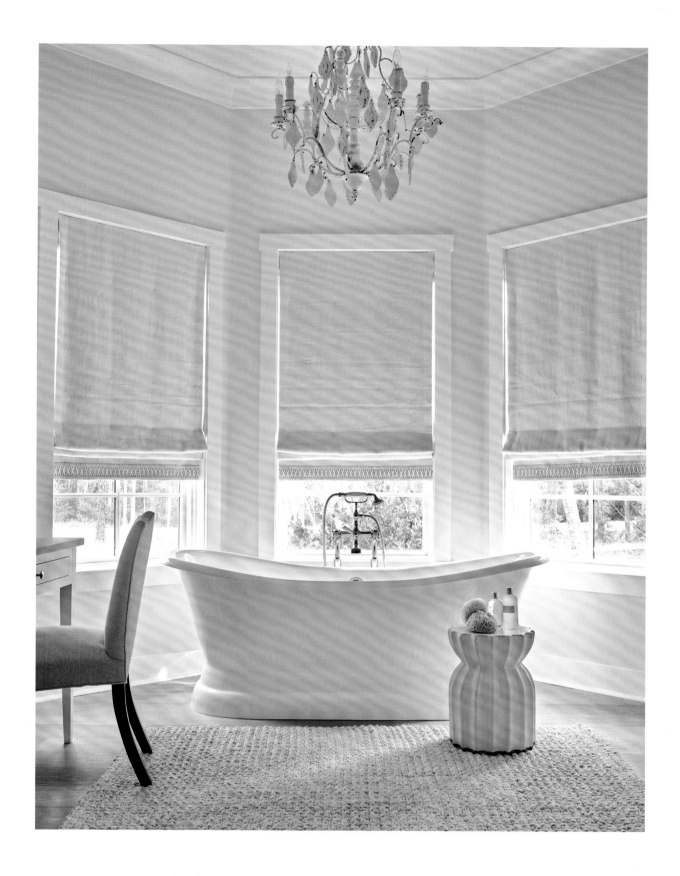

OPPOSITE AND ABOVE: In the white-on-white master bath, all is serene. A vignette on her vanity sums up the texture, materials, and color story. A gessoed wood chandelier adds a luminous piece of functional sculpture overhead. FOLLOWING PAGES, LEFT: From a stone fireplace surround to marble grape clusters, the master bedroom is full of gorgeous touch-me moments. FOLLOWING PAGES, RIGHT: Deep, soft seating and a knit wool throw create a cozy spot for curling up in front of the fire on a chilly Florida evening.

Touches of Romance

Every interior renovation begins with envisioning a world more beautiful to all our senses than the one right in front of our eyes. That's what designers do every day. Yet that's often difficult (or impossible) for the homeowners. Not for this couple. She appreciates and collects art, antiques, textiles, and porcelain as much for the way they feel in the hand as for their look and history. He's a passionate entrepreneur with a great enthusiasm for the design process. They love to travel. And just for fun—and for inspiration and future reference—they constantly collect intriguing materials and images of favorite rooms.

It came as no surprise, therefore, that when they found this Summerour and Associates-designed residence in Atlanta, they were able to see past its dark floors and dark wood paneling to its excellent bones and beautifully proportioned rooms. They knew that with lightening, brightening, and a little romancing, the spaces could be just as they imagined: soft, serene, organic, and full of misty tonalities.

Replacing the existing dark floors with antique French oak boards was the first step toward making their vision manifest. Then came painting the walls a pearlized shade of white. These two broad strokes immediately established the rooms as perfect backdrops for the couple's collections.

The living room had that extra-special something: a very high ceiling that captured the rippling of light dancing off the surface of the pool just beyond the windows. When I first saw the way those reflections shimmered and moved overhead, it reminded me of Venice, where the sun's rays mirroring off the canals seem to tinge everything with a touch of surreality. And just like there, in this room the air itself becomes palpable. To further enhance the effect, the client decided to layer the ceiling with multiple coats of high-gloss paint in a truly delicious

shade called "Healing Aloe." The result makes the space feel as if it's bathed under the glow of an Italian sky, rather than bound by the planes of the room.

How, where, and what we chose for the furnishings had much to do with either the piece's sentimental value—many that were picked up on the couple's travels play prominent roles in the décor—or its multifunctionality. A table of reclaimed Chinese elm, for example, serves as a dining table when surrounded by chairs. But when there's no dinner party on the menu and the chairs are moved back into their resting positions, the piece acts as a library table displaying the wife's trove of blue-and-white porcelain and extensive collection of monographs.

In a much-needed redo of the expansive kitchen, the existing dark space gave way to a combination of raw wood finishes, white-painted furniture, and an antique French limestone floor that together gave it a distinctly European flavor. It was the wife's idea to hang the linen curtain, a layer of softness, to serve as a movable wall and conceal the range during intimate meals with family and friends.

The bedroom contains a necessary touch of romance. And more than that, the room is truly ethereal: the contrasts of matte and shine, of soft and substantial, of voluptuousness and rigor, imbue it with a dreamy quality.

Reinvented to suit the owners' lifestyle and filled with their personal treasures, this home does what home should do: express a shared inner vision in every last touch.

PREVIOUS PAGES, RIGHT: For a couple that collects blue-and-white porcelains and ceramics from different eras and cultures, it made perfect sense to carry the color palette through the fabrics and finishes. The daybed in the loggia is dressed in linens from the trove the lady of the house has amassed over the years. OPPOSITE: In a lime-washed pecky cypress vestibule with shiplap walls, antique brackets hold pieces of her pewter collection. Infusing the space with additional charm is a gessoed twig chair. FOLLOWING PAGES, LEFT: The dining table regularly displays the couple's prized pieces, but it can be cleared and set for formal dinner parties. FOLLOWING PAGES, RIGHT: Lacquered a transcendent shade of blue-green, the ceiling reflects light off the pool beyond the windows.

Some Birds and Mammals of North America by Axel Amuchástegui

In the intimate, light-washed sunroom, a wall display of Chamberlain Worcester balances the sunburst mirror over the stone fireplace. At the heart of the room sits a Japanese pine tea table, another handy surface for displaying the treasures of their collections. The soft linen of the upholstery fabrics echoes the beautifully worn surfaces of the antique stone underfoot. FOLLOWING PAGES, LEFT: We painted the chair rail in the sunroom the same ethereal blue-green as the living/dining room ceiling to help tie the interior together. Her collection of Chamberlain Worcester spans 1783 to 1850. The Italian wall brackets are nineteenth-century. FOLLOWING PAGES, RIGHT: Vintage Gracie wallpaper panels fit perfectly into the mix.

OPPOSITE AND ABOVE: The kitchen encompasses the breakfast room, where the couple often has intimate meals with friends. A curtain wall of striped linen separates the cooktop from the seating area. FOLLOWING PAGES, LEFT: In the sitting room, an Italian chest of drawers circa 1840 takes pride of place next to a Directoire chair in antique linen velvet. FOLLOWING PAGES, RIGHT: In the master bedroom, a Picasso etching above the custom headboard draws the eye. Linen hangings frame the crown of the bed, which is dressed with a matelassé duvet.

ABOVE AND OPPOSITE: With the addition of steel-framed doors, we transformed the former pool house into her personal bath and private retreat. The French stone floor continues the blue-and-gray palette with a gray tumbled accent. She can pull a stool up to her custom vanity, housed neatly in one of the structure's niches. A Picasso hangs over her bath, which is custom finished on the exterior with car paint in her favorite Mercedes-Benz color.

Nature has her own kaleidoscope
of textures, infinitely varied and
profound. In this backyard, organic
tactile elements from lithic to
liquid to lush are shaped, structured,
and composed into a beautiful
life-enhancing landscape.

Sculpting Space

Interior design is the ultimate before-and-after story. What most people see is the beautiful post-transformation glow, but glimpsing whence each project comes really informs our understanding of the practical magic of design. This residence is a wonderful example of that dichotomy. It also offers a glance into a broader understanding of touch, one that encompasses the emotional resonance of objects passed from hand to hand and generation to generation.

The homeowners initially called me for help designing their forever home, then in its earliest stages of conception. Since completion was at least two years away, they decided to reinvent their existing home to make it more comfortable for the duration of their stay and to increase its eventual resale potential. That made good sense because their rooms—all hard lines, slick surfaces, and muddy colors—didn't feel welcoming. They wished for the exact opposite. The challenge here—highly achievable with a different palette of finishes, textures, and design details—was to create inviting spaces that were tangibly softer, much sexier, and much brighter.

What truly set the tone for reimagining their home, however, had nothing to do with the usual tools of design and decoration. The wife had an extraordinary collection of sculptures, maquettes, and medals created by her grandfather, the sculptor Henry Kreis, a German immigrant who had apprenticed with Paul Manship before launching his own artistic career. (As Manship's assistant, he worked on the statue of Prometheus at Rockefeller Center.) The couple had long been at a loss as to how to integrate this collection into their interiors. Needless to say, these remarkable pieces became a centerpiece of the renovation.

To refresh the rooms, we repainted them in a shade of white so ethereal it glows. To enhance an illusion of verticality under not-so-lofty ceilings, we corrected the drapery, hanging new panels high against the crown moldings. Throughout the home—but especially in the living

room—we used recessed shelving, pedestals, and other display options to transform the art, which was previously placed haphazardly in corners and even in storage, into a focal point.

In the living room, so many of the existing design elements were out of scale in relation to the dimensions of the overall volume: they were too small for the space. We retrofitted the fireplace surround; replaced otherwise uninviting contemporary black leather and chrome furnishings with soft, classic, transitional upholstery; and layered in sumptuous textures. For the overall palette, we developed a neutral spectrum that acts as a canvas for the terra-cotta maquettes, while pops of orange fabrics were added to accentuate the artworks.

The dining room posed a similar challenge when it came to scale. To induce a compelling change of character, we updated the lighting fixtures, changed the seating, and introduced a stately oval dining table and credenza. As major focal points within the room, we hung the wife's artist grandmother's works on paper and placed some of her grandfather's larger sculptures on pedestals.

The master bedroom also received a much-needed makeover. Because of the window placement, we opted to curtain all the walls with a diaphanous linen so the space felt warm and sensual. Through heightened contrast, the curtains and luxuriously layered bedding help to soften the contemporary lines of the upholstered leather bed.

The process of reinventing spaces always requires a deftness of hand. With a gentle touch, reminders of the past, and abundant texture, this renovation serves its purpose to provide embracing, welcoming surroundings for this family's foreseeable future.

PREVIOUS PAGES: On a cabinet of reclaimed Chinese elm, a sculpture by Henry Kreis, the lady of the house's artist grandfather, stands out. An alabaster lamp inserts a timeless note and another quality of white. OPPOSITE: A coffee table with hair-on-hide side rails doubles as an ottoman.

RIGHT: In the living room, quilted orange velvet pillows pick up on the terra-cotta color of her grandfather's maquettes. Along with the tulips, these elements form a triangular composition that brings the eye on an organized path through the interior of the room. FOLLOWING PAGES, LEFT: Introducing a display niche into a living room corner created a perfect spot for her grandfather's terra-cotta maquettes. FOLLOWING PAGES, RIGHT: Grasscloth wallcovering and a wood-bordered mosaic tile floor make a sophisticated yet understated background for displaying plaster studies.

PREVIOUS PAGES, LEFT: In the dining room, a large sculpture by her grandfather stands proudly next to works on paper by Patricia Kreis, her artist grandmother. PREVIOUS PAGES, RIGHT: Comfortable chairs wear custom linen slipcovers with contrasting hems. RIGHT: Everyone lives, works, and plays in the family room, which opens to the kitchen. A woodworking hobbyist with a workshop in the home, the gentleman of the house made the table and console. Adding elements of rustic craftsmanship to the wall are a pair of antique bread paddles and a pitchfork.

ABOVE AND OPPOSITE: The addition of a curtain wall that swathes the entire perimeter completely transformed the master bedroom from its former atmosphere of hard-edged modernity into the ultimate elegant, sensual cocoon of a private retreat. The vase picks up the rhythmic ripple of the fabric in another material and scale.

taste

As far as taste is concerned, there is a pachyderm in the boudoir, and his name is Marcel Proust. With that tea-soaked madeleine of legend, Proust forever married the sensory experience of savoring to the remembrance of things past—and therefore to the emotional life that we equate with home.

An aesthete of heightened sensitivities and remarkable powers of observation, Proust explored the cultivation of taste in all its guises, from pure and simple to beyond sophisticated, but especially as it relates to the art of living well. Living well has always been an individual art, one that expresses a personal understanding of and relationship to luxury and quality. We inevitably think of these two enhancements of daily life as interchangeable but they are, in fact, quite distinct.

Luxury has always been a form of indulgence, but it needn't be synonymous with expensive. What it must be is exquisite in its own right. Time, space, and light are the kinds of intangible extravagances that we all seek and rejoice in when we find them. But a perfect summer tomato is equally lavish. So is a blueberry fresh from the garden, a crisply ironed linen hand towel, or a glass that fits in the palm like a glove.

Good design delivers quality and luxury in tangible and intangible forms. A rigorously well-considered room includes a plan for comfort, which to my mind is the one luxury that's truly a necessity.

And as much as I would love to have everything in my surroundings be utterly, totally decadent, overabundance doesn't really make sense. A home requires a balance of the precious and the practical for livability. Regardless of the materials, place of origin, or craft behind each element that makes up our rooms, what ultimately determines whether we feel at home is the way each of the individual components relates to all the others. How well do rooms flow from one to the next? How does the light travel through the interior from sunrise to sunset? How seamlessly does a given object serve its function? Is the craftsmanship up to the intention? The indescribable feeling that comes with a perfect fit—a sensation that defies all expectations— emerges from the unique combination of the design details.

Our bodies feel quality. We instinctively know when we're swathed in exquisite sheeting or swaddled in the ultimate cashmere throw. Even if we can't put a name to the sensation or describe the difference, we aspire to it nonetheless. Such is the primal, instinctual understanding of beauty and luxury.

We all have a hierarchy of taste bred deep into our bones, for taste is what resonates with our inner chords of joy, beauty, and comfort. We continue to cultivate and refine it through constant education and experience.

Even as we develop an analytical superstructure and a critical language to parse taste, it remains, in essence, that visceral response we feel when we encounter what we love. Like home.

PREVIOUS PAGES: In a 1920s interior, silk damask wallpaper establishes a luminous background that speaks so appropriately to modern luxury. In such a space, mixing pieces from various periods, cultures, and styles makes ultimate sense. A blanc de chine figurine feels right at home with a Louis XV gilt wood mirror. OPPOSITE: In a lady's dressing room, a certain glamour should work its charms. A twentieth-century rock crystal lamp and a sleek Lucite tray atop a French Empire commode cast just the right spell. FOLLOWING PAGES: A walnut tester bed with a silk canopy feels true to the style of the room's original era, as does a chinoiserie lacquered table covered with an array of intriguing antique treasures. The silk charmeuse coverlet at the bed's foot recalls my grandmother's. PAGE 167: Organic elegance meets refinement on the lady of the house's blond macassar writing desk.

The Curatorial Eye

My favorite era of architecture, the 1920s, was a particularly fertile decade for the building of beauty across America. Our great houses from those years tend to contain rooms with pitch-perfect scale and proportion. More often than not, their architectural ornament—moldings, trims, pediments, and so on—demonstrates breathtaking refinement and restraint. Most wonderful of all is the dappled light that so often bathes the interiors. So when a call comes to create an up-to-date solution for this type of interior, who wouldn't leap at the chance? I certainly did when Maison de Luxe asked me to design the lady of the house's suite at Greystone, the historic Doheny Mansion in the heart of Beverly Hills.

On an earlier visit to the City of Angels, I had fallen in love with the estate, a mid-1920s Tudor Revival–style mansion designed by architect Gordon B. Kaufmann for Edward (Ned) and Lucy Doheny. The intrigue of this special place emanates partly from its backstory, which is so irresistibly Hollywood: the master of the property was done in during a shocking murder-suicide. Yet the house enthralls visitors because it encompasses incredibly gracious, elegant spaces amid gorgeous English-style gardens. The opportunity to reimagine one of the rooms would ignite any designer's ardor and imagination. But the chance to reinvent Mrs. Doheny's own suite—well, that just seemed almost too good to be true.

It turned out to be better.

In a showhouse, every design solution inevitably arises from one question: What would you do if you could do anything for yourself? As a sensualist, I am always attracted to spaces that are calm, inviting, and heavenly to the eye and to the touch. A suite like Mrs. Doheny's—bedroom, dressing room, and bath—should also be the ultimate timeless retreat. For that reason, I

used a soft tonal palette of creams, golds, and silvery grays, which evanesce into shimmer in the remarkable Los Angeles light. And because the interior architecture sets such a high standard, the only appropriate response was to match the surroundings with exceptionally luxurious furnishings and lavish fabrics and accessories. In other words, *custom* to the nth degree.

Reinstating a level of luxury, craftsmanship, and quality mirroring the house's original construction—that's the point where my passion met my professionalism. The drapery fabric—linen with silk embroidery—raised the bar in decadence. It also provided inspiration for everything else in these rooms, including walls covered in de Gournay silk damask paper and some exceptional furnishings provided by Dessin Fournir, Therien, and many others. A bespoke Kyle Bunting hide rug with an abstracted version of the curtain embroidery pattern mimicked the pediments of the original built-in étagères.

For such an expansive suite, the rooms feel extraordinarily intimate. At their heart is a silk-spun cocoon of a four-poster encircled with sumptuous hangings and a pleated silk canopy.

Layers of gorgeous linens dress the bed. On top of it all is a modern rendition of my grandmother's 1920s silk charmeuse comforter, which was part of my childhood and my children's. We loved it and her so much, we kept it until the very last shred.

OPPOSITE: The glamour that pervaded the 1920s infuses her rooms with its distinctive perfume. Her desktop hosts a gorgeous array of objects that layer new with old, including a nineteenth-century English writing set. Underfoot, a custom hair-on-hide rug unfurls with a pattern inspired by the embroidered drapery panels. FOLLOWING PAGES, LEFT: An Empire console adds to the sophistication of the space. FOLLOWING PAGES, RIGHT: Lush peonies in bronze vases bring the floral ornament of the Japanese low table to life.

PREVIOUS PAGES, LEFT: In her dressing room, a spectacular slab of blue Bahia stone tops the vanity table. PREVIOUS PAGES, RIGHT: Amid rock crystal obelisks, vintage crystal perfume bottles, and a vintage silver box, an Italian giltwood mirror takes center stage. A custom hide rug softens the floor. ABOVE: A midcentury rock crystal lamp and Lucite and crystal objects introduce a soigné allure and an understated glitter to this corner of her dressing area. OPPOSITE: Behind the furs and all the couture, a Dorothy Draper–designed wallpaper infuses the interior of her closet with a bold, idiosyncratic period charm. A fur throw nonchalantly drapes over the end of the chaise longue. As for the ball gown, it's Oscar de la Renta . . . of course!

Point of View

It all began with the land, the sea, and a sophisticated European sensibility—and a made-just-for-them house on a site in Greenwich, Connecticut, with a spectacular view of Long Island Sound. At the time they began this project, my clients were in the first phase of young family life. They had lived in many places and traveled the world over. Collectors of fine art and antiquities, they had long cared about quality and tradition. He grew up with parents who made frequent purchases in the fine auction houses of the world, and who taught him to do the same. When we met, he had also formed long-standing relationships with antiques dealers in Holland who would regularly send their latest acquisitions for perusal. The couple would arrive at my office with stacks of catalogs from the upcoming auctions at Christie's and Sotheby's, announcing that we would be buying rugs at the sales in London next week. But the overriding design philosophy was that the house be livable, because for both of them, the children came first, and the overall design needed to emanate comfort and warmth.

The house was situated to make the most of the available vistas, as one would expect of its architect, Keith Summerour of Summerour and Associates, who had known the couple for several years prior to their purchase of the property. One of the best parts of this project was Keith's insistence on building the strongest team possible. Landscape architect Jeremy Smearman of Planters Inc. captured the panoramas that incorporated the original orchard and great lawn sweeping down to the water. Intended to be the clients' forever house, the

Normandy-style structure was three years in the making. No detail was left to chance, as is reflected in the materials and finishes throughout: large, multipane, steel-framed windows; antique French limestone floors; and a traditional slate roof all personify permanence.

As much as my clients' taste leaned toward formality, their overall lifestyle was inherently casual. They asked for all of the rooms to be livable, even those displaying their pre-Columbian art, Han dynasty ceramics, Mirós, and Picassos. They felt strongly that the children (and dogs) should be able to inhabit each and every room, with no space deemed too precious or off-limits. Accordingly, they requested there be no formal dining room. Instead, they opted for a family room, dining room, and kitchen, all in combination.

The dining area, with its integrated banquette and farmhouse table, overlooks the indoor pool and offers a view of the water. Even the living room reflects full-on family style—and the dog's favorite chair has already been re-covered several times. In the paneled library, off the formal living room, the children can often be found with their father, either engaged in a game of chess or doing homework at the massive antique partners desk.

In a home that includes many exceptional views by design, the indoor pool—used with great gusto in all seasons—may be the most unexpected of all.

But even here, as so often happens, the family's lifestyle choices have fueled the design and decoration. And that's the point, in their point of view.

PAGE 177: In the foyer, an antique Dutch chair cozies up to a Charles II oak chest. PREVIOUS PAGES, LEFT: From around and on high, light flows into an unexpectedly intimate living room. Beautiful objects and fine art, including several Mirós, add luster to the space. An antique Persian carpet introduces lush pattern underfoot. PREVIOUS PAGES, RIGHT: A focal piece hanging over the stone hearth, a Miró infuses its bold forms and colors into the living room. Han Dynasty pots from their collection grace the coffee table. Nail-studded upholstered tabourets offer extra pull-up seating when required. OPPOSITE: With a Tang dynasty horse, a contemporary crystal lamp, and a Picasso print, this antique Dutch sideboard hosts a summit between the ancient and the modern.

ABOVE: In the powder room, an antique Italian marble sink is one of several unique flourishes. OPPOSITE: Under a soaring two-story ceiling, raw silk burlap curtain panels warm up a grand stair hall. FOLLOWING PAGES: A kitchen-side sitting room serves as a second living room. To withstand everyday wear and tear, the rug is heavily textured. Chenille upholstery fabric offers similar practical beauty.

ABOVE: The family didn't want a formal enclosed dining room, so they share meals in another room off the kitchen. The table is a Dutch antique. OPPOSITE: With concrete countertops and an antique iron chandelier, the kitchen incorporates an unexpected mix of materials. FOLLOWING PAGE, LEFT: The library looks into one of the many gardens. For an interesting textural contrast at the windows, custom printed raw silk panels frame linen Roman shades. Choice pieces from the couple's collection of pre-Columbian pottery sit proudly on the shelves. FOLLOWING PAGE, RIGHT: Steel windows and French doors open to a spectacular waterfront view from this Greenwich home.

ABOVE: A nineteenth-century stone beauty rises gracefully against a boxwood backdrop. OPPOSITE: The indoor pool is a fun family play space in all seasons. FOLLOWING PAGES: The lawn of this Greenwich home sweeps all the way down to the water.

scent

THE GREAT AMERICAN HOUSE GIL SCHAFER

It fascinates me to no end that there is such a calling as a professional "nose." In another life, I might wish to be one. The myth of a house that possesses the fragrance of a dream home isn't a myth at all. It's a verifiable reality, as any real estate broker will attest. Citrus, fresh-cut pine, and cinnamon are just a few of the scents that professionals advise sellers to use as they help put prospective buyers in the right mood to imagine their lives within the space. Every single one of us follows our nose to the seat of our most trusted bellwether instinct: home.

I have visceral memories of so many of the houses I've visited based on their individual aromas—particularly those great houses of England and Europe that I have toured as part of my time spent abroad. If design history has its own defining aroma, the scent of wax on furniture may well be it. Add to that alluring effect the perfume of David Austin roses from the garden casually arranged upon the table, and it's a combination for the ages, one that will always say "country house" to me. The aroma of lamb roasting in the oven conjures up the image of Sunday suppers at my grandmother's: her beautifully laid table, crisply starched linens, sparkling crystal, polished silver, and gleaming china— the family members gathered around.

There are many tangible intangibles that contribute to creating the comforts we think of as home. But among them, scent has a particular and peculiar power. Just from a purely animal-instinct point of view, smell is a primal force, a trigger to so many tantalizing aspects of existence: awareness, attraction, safety, and so on. From our earliest days, we learn to relax into calmness through the recognition of a personal fragrance, especially when it's combined in some mysterious way with the rhythm of a heartbeat, the sound of a particular voice, the form of a familiar face, and the touch of a beloved hand, blanket, or other soft thing. As children, we grow increasingly conscious of the many aromas, exceptional and everyday, that are, or seem to be, intrinsic to our lives at home. We grow up to follow our noses into the kitchen, the bath, the garden, and, eventually, the wider world.

Each place, each season, each person and celebration has its own distinctive bouquets that waft deeply into memory's recesses, and that startle us again each time they reappear in our consciousness. We all associate scents with time, place, and pleasure. I remember so vividly how we went through the house to disperse its contents after my grandfather passed away. On the corner of his desk, I discovered a bottle of my grandmother's perfume, Chanel No. 19. He had kept it there, all those years after her death, to remind him of her because the power of that scent and the memories he associated with it were so profound.

We comprehend the source of each of these bouquets in terms of color, form, and texture. Peonies—in particular, white peonies—are my favorite flower. I especially love them stem upon stem, crowded to bursting in a simple glass vase on the coffee table in my living room.

The headiness of a floral fragrance, the way a sumptuous arrangement captivates the eye in the daylight or candlelight, the decadent sensuality of the blooms at the point of overripeness—that's the scent of design to me, and so much more.

PREVIOUS PAGES: The scent of freshly laundered, starched, and ironed linens is really second to none. FOLLOWING PAGES: When everyday items bear personal meaning, they offer the balm of memories. On my dressing table, my grandmother's silver hairbrush and mirror and my own perfume bottles take on starring roles.

Aromatherapy

Scent is something we experience viscerally—and as an emotional trigger. Like light, it also serves as a mood enhancer. And for me, as for many people, it can be a form of joy and of peace. That's why I focus on using fragrance along with all the elements of décor to create sensual living environments with a lightness of being. The tang of citrus, the ambrosia of lilies of the valley: these and so many other aromas, from earthy loam to lovely lavender, are the perfumes that bring us home.

When the homeowners purchased this house on Lake Chatuge, Georgia, the interiors were dark, to say the least—as dark as the surroundings were light and scent-laden. There was deep orange stone on some walls, burgundy-colored mahogany trim everywhere, a stained cherrywood floor, and heavy red draperies that felt oppressive. These clients asked for light, bright, and white spaces with a collected sensibility. Although definitely unexpected in a lake house, these aims suited the wife's vision of a second home imbued with harmonious calm. And while the couple took a relaxed approach to the redesign, they also had a hard deadline and needed the transformation to occur in fewer than six months, having closed in November and planning to be in by Easter.

Lacking the time to do any significant structural renovations to the interior architecture or replace existing fireplaces or many of the fixtures, we worked around the problems. First, we stripped down the rooms completely and utilized lime paints and washes to

transform the surfaces—walls, floors, antique beams, dark-paneled ceilings, and—somewhat unusually—stone. We even lime-washed the existing antler chandeliers. The effect of that one bold stroke was nothing short of amazing, similar to when the sun breaks through the clouds. We then replaced dated and dark granite counters and added shiplap to the fireplace walls in the master bath, where we also introduced a freestanding tub.

The couple brought not one piece of furniture with them to this house, so it served as a blank canvas. We selected all the new options for sumptuousness, function, and durability, and we slipcovered the dining chairs and upholstered almost all the pieces in solution-dyed acrylic fabrics for ease of maintenance. For contrast with all the rough-hewn textures, we layered in softness by employing natural hides, richly woven Moroccan rugs, and crisp linens, which energized the quiet palette with a high degree of texture and textural pattern.

We also selected the necessary accoutrements and accessories (everything from pillows and decorative objects to tableware and bedding) that this home required.

When we're given free rein and trusted down to the last detail, we can create interiors that encourage a lightness of being.

PREVIOUS PAGES: A bowl full of lemons adds zest and piquancy to any tabletop, rustic or refined. OPPOSITE: In a room where sparseness of decoration is the watchword, every element of architecture and each piece of furniture takes on sculptural significance. FOLLOWING PAGES, LEFT: A wall composition of large and small European mounts helps to bring this two-story space back to human scale. FOLLOWING PAGES, RIGHT: A graphic rug anchors the gentleman's office; its banded motif recurs in various materials and at various scales.

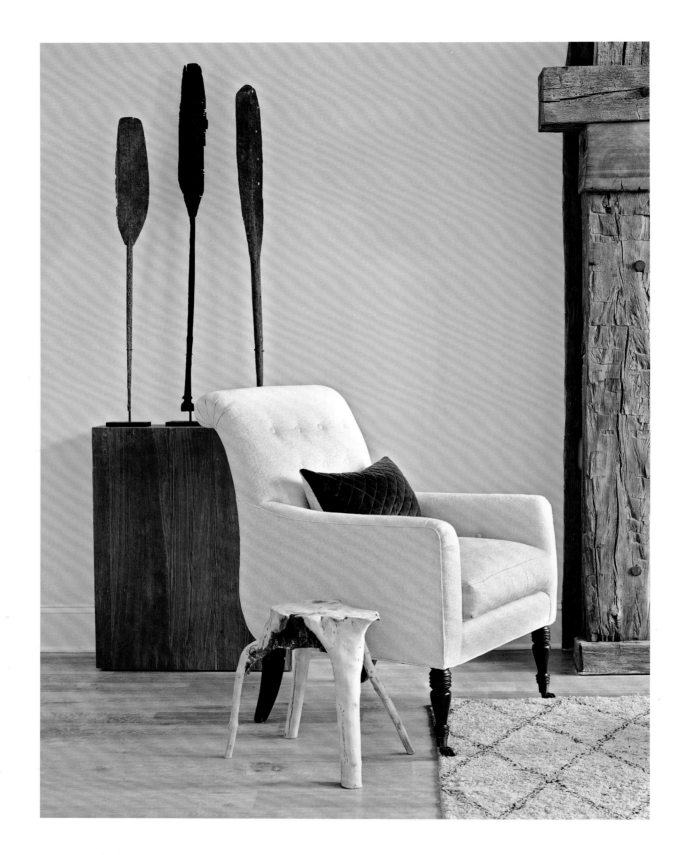

ABOVE: In the living room, a driftwood drinks table introduces an organic element to this mélange of the refined and the rustic. OPPOSITE: Chinese calligraphy brushes on the coffee table echo the shape of the antlers used throughout the home. FOLLOWING PAGES, LEFT: Antique antler shelves add form and texture. FOLLOWING PAGES, RIGHT: To transform this house in a tight time frame, we gave all the existing elements (including the living room's antler chandelier) a light, lime-wash finish. A Moroccan rug adds texture, softness, and a linear graphic element underfoot; those lines repeat, crisply, in the coffee table's iron base.

DESIGNERS AT HOME

RONDA RICE CARMAN

ALBERTO PINTO *Table Settings*

LIVING IN STYLE LONDON

PREVIOUS PAGES, LEFT: With their heady, intoxicating aroma and fabulous texture, spring peonies from the garden add another layer of emotion to the bedroom. PREVIOUS PAGES, RIGHT: On a bed sumptuously dressed with Italian linens, the gracious double flange of the pillowcases beckons against a deeply tufted headboard. OPPOSITE: In the master bath, the bather feels embedded in the lake views; a hide rug atop a lime-washed floor enhances comfort. ABOVE: Reams of linen encircle the bay of the guest room, creating column-like elements that frame the lake view. Embroidered linen duvet covers and shams, quilted coverlets, and a knitted throw create a textural harmony.

Scents and Sensibilities

Scents, sights, and sounds all remind us that nature is our greatest sensualist. So why not embrace her marvels with architecture and design? This was the goal of my client, the visionary behind the ideal place that he named Las Catalinas. In this planned town, situated on the Pacific Coast in Costa Rica, he set out to create a magical community that would honor his mantra of sustainability and utilize 1,200 acres of untamed wilderness in the most mindful way.

My client commissioned architect Lew Oliver to design this H-shaped, three-story house for him and his family. One of the first structures in Las Catalinas, it opens itself to the environment in the most welcoming way, with an ocean-facing courtyard from which to contemplate the beauty and beat of the surf, and with symmetrical loggias on the first and second floors that welcome a bouquet of exotic perfumes, which enchant the breezes and make the air there feel palpable.

The client specifically wanted the house to frame the ocean views and vistas, and to incorporate ample open living areas so the scent of the sea could dance through the spaces. Each room needed to be intimate enough for family living yet expansive enough to accommodate the large parties that this couple, so adept at gracious entertaining, love to host. Above all, they wanted the house to have a sense of place. Their goal was to create an overall sensibility that was respectful of, but not beholden to, Costa Rica's Spanish-influenced design traditions. For the owners' purposes, it seemed appropriate to brighten the interior finishes so typical of Costa Rican homes, where darker woods usually prevail. "Light and white" became the catchphrase of the day. We opted for an understated palette of neutrals underscored by small accents of color. To quietly energize the calm palette, we infused the spaces with texture.

Early in the design process, we headed to the Costa Rican capital of San José to search for materials, furnishings, and craftspeople. Our finds included manufacturers for surfaces like the Cuban tile used for flooring and in the baths as well as the Coralina stones that pave the courtyard and loggias. But we were not so lucky with the furnishings, so we expanded our search to Mexico City for the necessary antiques, art, furniture, and accessories. It was then that the interiors started coming into focus.

Gorgeously patterned fabric panels drape the living room windows, and antique textiles add boldness and history here and there. Since the couple wanted the house to be used, and used well, it was important that the upholstery be covered in family-friendly materials. We chose slipcovers in outdoor fabrics that felt and looked elegant yet could withstand the daily use that comes with significant entertaining. Being introduced to extraordinary artisans in Mexico who were reinterpreting traditional crafts for more contemporary tastes proved pivotal. As a result, we were able to select hand-embroidered bedding and napkins, and custom tabletop décor, including place mats woven with ceramic leaves, antique etched-glass hurricanes, and handblown glassware.

In this very special place surrounded by wilderness, the design of this house is intended to gratify all the senses—down to the last perfectly aromatic detail.

PREVIOUS PAGES: On Costa Rica's Pacific coast, a dramatic sunset heightens all the senses. OPPOSITE: Creeping fig covers walls that frame a doorway to the poolside lounge area. FOLLOWING PAGES, LEFT: For her husband's birthday, the lady of the house commissioned a sculpture of sea turtles hatching on the beach. While local artisans crafted some of the furnishings and architectural elements on site, we had to travel to Mexico City for accessories such as the turned-wood bowl and baskets. FOLLOWING PAGES, RIGHT: Like an Italian campanile, a three-story tower rises over the open-air poolside dining grotto.

PREVIOUS PAGES: Open to nature on two sides, a Coralina-floored loggia is the ultimate romantic breakfast room. An oversized wood bowl just outside the doorway holds flip-flops and other accoutrements of beach life. The curtains sway in the breeze day and night.

RIGHT: The first element selected for this room, the hand-blocked curtain panels introduce an eye-catching pattern language. An antique Suzani draped across the back of the sofa and embroidered pillows broaden the graphic range. With a pair of oversized club chairs, the seating area provides a host of visual and actual comforts.

PREVIOUS PAGES, LEFT: Exotic fruits bring color, texture, and a wonderful mingling of aromas to the table.
PREVIOUS PAGES, RIGHT: White-glazed pottery from San Miguel de Allende enhances the table's more rustic elements.
OPPOSITE: The indoor breakfast area connects to the kitchen. Cool and quiet, it features a Cuban tile floor, slipcovered wicker chairs from France, and a lamp made from an antique glass orb filled with blue water. ABOVE: Glass-fronted cabinets highlight handmade Mexican tableware. Lamps against the tile backsplash add layers of light to the kitchen.

OPPOSITE: In a refined color palette, traditional Mexican embroidered textiles elevate an age-old craft technique to a new level. ABOVE: With an arched and louvered window that opens to the scent of the sea air, this alfresco master bath provides an intimate, refreshing sanctuary.

A Whiff of History

We interior designers love to describe the homes we create as both timeless and timely, especially those that we shepherd into existence from scratch. And we mean it. It's a worthy challenge on every level to deliver rooms that look as if they've always been there yet appear to have come into being uniquely for those who dwell in them. Such enduring spaces are what architect Peter Block and I set out to realize for this couple, their three teenage sons, and their Labrador retriever, in a from-the-ground-up residence that they and others have referred to as "the new-old house." But despite a feeling of age, there are no musty odors here, just the comforting aromas of lit hearths, a well-used kitchen, and the lightest linger of wax and polish.

A bit of a hybrid, the two-story structure locates all the common areas and the master suite on the ground floor, with the boys' bedrooms and guest quarters upstairs. The proportions of windows and doors—inspired, according to Peter Block, by the residential architecture of Sir Edwin Lutyens and the English Arts and Crafts movement—hint at old-world sensibilities. The high-ceilinged and light-washed interior architecture and the materials and finishes all skew toward modern, though they're classic, too. In the main living areas, plaster walls play host to cast-stone mantels, floor-to-ceiling fenestration, and generously transomed French doors. High overhead, nineteenth-century oak beams add history and patina.

The vast great room, windowed along both sides, spans the central core of the home. At one end live the kitchen and family/gathering room; at the other, the master suite and library. The three main living areas—great room, library, and gathering room—open to a loggia the family uses year-round. All are multifunctional living spaces that easily accommodate the casual lifestyle that typifies this family. They love to entertain and do so frequently, but since they're not much for the formal dinner party, they opted to do without a separate dining room.

The great room contains three seating arrangements. One, an open dining space, abuts the kitchen (and its tantalizing aromas) and incorporates a banquette and a long farm table. The second, in the great room's heart, features back-to-back sofas anchored by long, low

bookshelves that give off the subtle scent of books. The third provides a more intimate conversational nest in front of the fireplace, where the fragrance of burning logs entices.

Throughout the interior, a deeply considered layering of textures, materials, and finishes offers an ineffable whiff of the idea of rooms long ago. We carefully considered each piece of furniture, every textile, and all the lighting and accessories for functionality, classic appeal, and comfort. A Northern European–inspired palette of taupes, ivories, and earth tones reinforces a timeless feeling; the colors are soft, the materials forgiving.

In the kitchen, texture tells the story. Lime-washed surfaces lend character and patina to what is obviously a contemporary space. A custom plaster range hood acts as functional sculpture and reinforces the old-world theme.

In the family room—both a breakfast setting and a gathering area—the texture story twists again. Here, long linen window panels contrast with a tactile jute rug, an antique velvet sofa, and lime-washed shiplap walls.

In the master suite, a far more feminine air prevails with embroidered fabrics, sumptuous bedding, and curvaceous upholstery. Through architecture and design, a sense of time past inhabits this brand-new residence.

The home lives the way the family does: simply and graciously, with a fire laid in every room, even in the summer months. Such is time's perfume—and the scents that speak of the comforts of home.

PREVIOUS PAGES: Full of hydrangeas, an antique metal bucket brings a rustic refinement to a tabletop. OPPOSITE: The dining area is part and parcel of the main living room. Reclaimed beams overhead and antique dining chairs impart a feeling of history. FOLLOWING PAGES: The living room's opposite end houses a conversation group in front of the hearth. For versatility, we used three small coffee tables instead of one large one. A textural bouclé fabric covers the club chairs. Flanking the fireplace are storage cabinets for logs.

In the breakfast room, floor-to-ceiling linen panels with contrasting fabric borders infuse the room with understated pattern and elements of almost architectural verticality. A sculptural table base inserts interesting curves into a space where linear graphic components feel dominant. From the rough to the ultrasmooth, a broad spectrum of textures adds tactile interest and visual personality.

The family room shares space with the breakfast room yet offers an interesting contrast. "Virtually indestructible" was my mantra here, as befits a house with three active boys and two black Labs. Thanks to a mix of materials and fabrics that are neutral in color and forgiving in every possible way, this room will withstand time's test. Set into a wall niche, an antique wheat thresher becomes an architectural element.

ABOVE: In the library, an antique writing desk holds favorite objects, including vintage writing boxes and an inkwell in the shape of a dog's head. OPPOSITE: An intimate space designed for two, this room holds generous bergères for reading quietly in front of the fire. At the windows are Italian linen curtain panels, a bold graphic element in an otherwise understated interior.

RIGHT: The custom plaster range hood
becomes the centerpiece of the kitchen,
and a sculptural focal point; a classic French
griddle pan takes pride of place above it.
The Calacatta Viola marble countertops and
backsplash create an art-like moment; the
marble's veining introduces an extraordinary
effect of movement into the space, as
well as gorgeous variations of color and tone.
FOLLOWING PAGES, LEFT: Antique earthenware
bowls add a patina honestly achieved.
FOLLOWING PAGES, RIGHT: Under a lime-
washed pecky cypress ceiling, outdoor living
and dining areas open directly off the
interior and run the length of the living room.

The F[...]

The Florence Academy of Art

ART AND LOVE IN
RENAISSANCE ITALY

VERANDA   THE ART OF
OUTDOOR LIVING

FROM THE LAND   The Architecture of Backen [...]

assouline.com

LITTLE BLACK DRESS

ANDRÉ LEON TALLEY
PHOTOGRAPHS BY ADAM KUEHL

Skira Rizzoli

A Sense of Beauty

Each of us has our own idea of home. Often, it has to do with a particular look and with the practical, pragmatic things we need or desire for comfortable everyday living. These are important. Critical, in fact. Yet there's more. Many of us also harbor deep within ourselves an ideal of home, a dream of feelings and meanings rather than concepts or styles. For me, this ideal of home is what interior design is all about, and why the realms of beauty that it is capable of creating matter so very much.

I crave order out of chaos. That, for me, is beauty's essence. It is also the reason I am an interior designer.

Design is sensual on every level. It is experiential. It is about extracting the most and the best of every single solitary moment down to the physical last detail of behavior and environment. Designers have a gift for intuiting and envisioning what others find difficult to express and imagine. We think in a million different directions simultaneously, correlating and editing innumerable options into possibilities that serve the functions of everyday living and the goal of doing so in an environment of particular beauty. We can walk into a preexisting space and imagine its reinvention. We can look at a set of outlines on a piece of paper and know what each room will look and feel like in three

dimensions and how the rooms will connect to one another. We understand the activities of life in each of those spaces, so we are able to picture them fully furnished to function at their best for various purposes (cooking, entertaining, gathering, sleeping, playing), layered to the last accessory and nth detail. We feel the quality of these experiences: overall, exceptional, everyday. We translate that sensory overload into terms of beauty that serve the civilized way we all aspire to live.

Fleeting sensations may be just that—fleeting. But still they can catch us, hold us out of time, and take us out of ourselves and beyond the daily distractions. And so I believe in the power of beauty. It enhances life in ways well beyond words.

No day should pass without our experiencing a sense of beauty in one form or another, even for a moment. A glimpse of the possibility of perfection. Something wonderful against the skin. A snatch of melody. A whiff of perfume. A taste of happiness.

PAGE 246: My living room coffee table is home to a constantly changing landscape of moments of beauty that catch my eye. PREVIOUS SPREAD, LEFT: I'm a great believer in using the pieces I love, for they carry forward a lifetime of memories. On my dining table, a Waterford crystal vase pairs neatly with Match pewter bowls and my mother's silver candlesticks. PREVIOUS SPREAD, RIGHT: My grandmother's sterling water goblets always dress my table. On the wall hangs an array of drawings collected throughout the years in Florence. OPPOSITE: While flowers with crisp hints of greens, like these dahlias, feel like the freshest of finishing touches.

Acknowledgments

As a designer, I am entrusted by my clients with one of the greatest responsibilities there is, that of creating a home. I take that task seriously and listen carefully as they initially describe that place they will inhabit—the house that holds their hopes and dreams, their present and their future. It is the ultimate expression of who and what they are. Home is much more than a place to me; it is a feeling. A complicated and beautiful amalgamation of all the senses and what memories are ultimately made of. Over the last two and a half decades, I have been privileged to design many such homes, and there will never be enough words to adequately express my gratitude to both my clients and all those people who helped me to achieve that.

In life I've found that there is often an "aha" moment when you least expect it—one that plants a seed and propels you forward. For me, that moment came in the brilliant form of Jill Cohen, who one day said, "You're ready." Without her, this book would never have been. For your friendship, support, and unending counsel, Jill, thank you. You continually give more than you ever should, tirelessly and graciously. To the oh-so-eloquent Judith Nasatir, thank you for helping me find my voice and my story. To Doug Turshen and Steve Turner, for your unwavering eye for exquisite composition, not to mention extraordinary patience with endless changes, my deepest thanks. And to everyone at Rizzoli, specifically Charles Miers, thank you for giving me the opportunity to bring my work to the world. Aliza Fogelson, I am forever indebted to you for your gentle guidance and unerring attention to detail.

I'll never forget the day my work was first published; thank you, Clinton Smith, for everything! Your friendship and years of support have meant the world to me. Sincere thanks go to all the magazine editors who have championed my work over the years, including Elizabeth Ralls, Newell Turner, Dara Caponigro, Doretta Sperduto, Michael Boodro, Ann Maine, Pamela Pierce, Leslie Newsom Rascoe, Pamela Jaccarino, and Sophie Dow Donelson. I continue to be humbled each and every time I see my work in print.

I am a firm believer in the team approach and feel so tremendously blessed to be a part of many wonderful collaborations with talented architects and builders. My profound gratitude goes to Summerour and Associates, Peter Block Architects, D. Stanley Dixon Architect, Jeffrey Dungan Architects, T.S. Adams Studio, Laura Howard Architect, Harrison Design, Lew Oliver Inc., The

Garrett Group, Young and Meathe Custom Homes, Derazi Homes, and Luis Diego Calzada.

The completion of any project, no matter how large or small, would not be possible without my dedicated team at Beth Webb Interiors. "The Girls," as I so fondly call them, give their all to make certain there is no "i" left undotted, no "t" left uncrossed. Thank you, Mary Clare Holm, Whitney Ray, and Courtney Godwin, for making the BWI world go 'round. Without you, I would be lost.

Elliott Erwitt said, "The whole point of taking pictures is so you don't have to explain things with words." To my photographers, thank you for putting your hearts and souls into bringing these interiors to life through your camera lenses. To my principal photographer, Emily Followill, thank you for your artistic eye and poetic interpretations. Erica George Dines, Mali Azima, Bill Abranowicz, Gemma and Andrew Ingalls, Laura Resen, and Lisa Romerein, it was truly my pleasure to work with you all.

Whether "God is in the details" or the devil is, I'm not sure—probably a bit of both. But I am certain of one thing: without our many partners, collaborators, and colleagues, our job would be much more difficult. We remain indebted to you all: Bungalow Classic, Ainsworth-Noah, Jerry Pair, Grizzel and Mann, Travis and Company, A. Tyner Antiques, Holland and Sherry, Parc Monceau, Robuck, Trellis Design, Tecnosedia, Raymond Goins, Marmi Natural Stone, Morgan Creek Cabinet Company, Block and Chisel, ROMABIO, R. Hughes, Edgar-Reeves, Mrs. Howard, Eleanor Roper, Joanne Sims, Calhoun Design and Metalworks, Leontine Linens, Schumacher, Waterworks, Rob Alexander, Terry Greenfield, Circa Lighting, and Merida. To my creative team, John Lineweaver and Laurie Salmore, thank you for seeing me more clearly than I ever could. There are so many more to be thanked and not enough space in which to do so. A very special thank you to three people in particular, without whom I would never have become a designer: Bruz Clark, Chip Cheatham, James Kreuzberg— thank you for believing in me.

To my wonderful family, who have supported me through thick and thin (sometimes more thick than thin), I owe you everything. To the memory of my mother, you have my love and gratitude; I only wish you were still here to share this! And to my dear Chuck, with whom I am my best self, thank you for your unconditional love, for finding me and giving me the family and sense of home I didn't even know I was missing. To our children, Taylor, Graeme, Charlie, and Gray (and the furry one, Catalina), having you all around me is the purest definition of home.

Photography Credits

All photography by Emily J. Followill Photography with the exception of the following images:

William Abranowicz: pages 129, 132–133, 136

Mali Azima Photography: pages 8, 178–179, 182–186, 188, 192–193

Erica George Dines Photography: pages 60, 63–65, 67–68, 70–83, 215–216, 218–221, 224–225, 233–239, 242–245

Andrew and Gemma Ingalls, The Epicures: pages 177, 180, 187, 189–191

Laura Resen Photography: pages 222–223, 226–229

Lisa Romerein Photographs: pages 160, 163–165, 167, 169–175

Matt Wong Photography: page 101

Project Credits

LOVE AT FIRST GLANCE (page 22)
Original Architect: Philip Trammell Shutze
First Renovation Architect:
   Spitzmiller and Norris, Inc.
Second Renovation Architect:
   D. Stanley Dixon Architect
Contractor: Y.M. Derazi Custom Homes

SIGHT LINES (page 38)
Architect: Presley Architecture
Interior Architecture: Peter Block Architects
Contractor: Young and Meathe Custom Homes

CALL OF THE WILD (page 66)
Architect: Michael G. Imber Architects

BLUE NOTES (page 84)
Architect: DreamBuilt
Contractor: DreamBuilt

SOFT FOCUS (page 104)
Architect: Dream Finders Homes
Contractor: Dream Finders Homes

TOUCHES OF ROMANCE (page 128)
Architect: Summerour and Associates
Landscape Architect: Summerour
   and Associates

THE CURATORIAL EYE (page 166)
Architect: Gordon B. Kaufmann

POINT OF VIEW (page 176)
Architect: Summerour and Associates
Interior Architecture: Summerour
   and Associates
Landscape Architect: Planters, Inc.
Contractor: SBE Builders Inc.

SCENTS AND SENSIBILITIES (page 214)
Architect: Lew Oliver Nest

A WHIFF OF HISTORY (page 230)
Architect: Peter Block Architects
Interior Architecture: Peter Block Architects
Landscape Architect: Howard Design Studio
Contractor: Y.M. Derazi Custom Homes

First published in the United States of America in 2017
by Rizzoli International Publications, Inc.
300 Park Avenue South
New York, NY 10010
www.rizzoliusa.com

Copyright © 2017 by Beth Webb
Photography credits appear on page 254.

Designed by Doug Turshen with Steve Turner

2017 2018 2019 2020 / 10 9 8 7 6 5 4 3 2 1

Distributed in the U.S. trade by Random House, New York

Printed in China

ISBN-13: 978-0-8478-6020-3

Library of Congress Control Number: 2017933363